This book was created for all of you who enjoy giving gifts to others. Your gift-giving pleasure will be enhanced as you discover page after page of unique and exciting gift wrap designs for everyone on your list. The photos are beautiful and there are detailed instructions with every project.

Creating this book has been most enjoyable for me because of several wonderful friends who contributed many of the gift wraps it contains. I asked them to wrap a gift with their own special ideas, and you will be delighted with the fabulous packages they have designed for you!

Something extra special is in this book that you and your children are sure to enjoy. I asked twelve children to actually do the projects we wanted to feature in the "Kids" section. You will see the most terrific gift wrap for kids that has ever been published!

A special, special thank you to all of you who made this book so unique! I know all who read it will be inspired by the many new ideas!

ENJOY!!

Judi

CREATING THE VERY BEST
Giftwrapping

CONTENTS

FROM THE GARDEN

Adorn your packages with flowers from your garden. They are dried by hanging upside down, in a dark place for several weeks.

MATERIALS NEEDED

Solid color wrapping paper
Dried flowers
4 yards of 4" wide tulle netting
Wire

INSTRUCTIONS

1. Choose a beautiful paper and wrap your gift following the instructions on page 24.

2. Make your dried flower mini bouquet from any flowers you have on hand. Marsha used silver dusty miller, 3 rosebuds, 6 sprigs of lavender and a cluster of statice. Tie securely with twine or wire.

3. Wrap a length of 4" wide tulle netting twice around your box and tie a knot at the top. Leave one end 6" long and the other end 12" long, cutting ends on the diagonal. Pull tulle netting apart to cover more area on your box.

4. Wire your dried flowers over the knot on the tulle; then tie the tulle around the flower stems and knot.

5. The darling tulle net puffs are easy to make. Cut a length of 4" wide tulle 20" long and lay it flat on a table. Now "walk" your fingers right up the middle to gather. Tie it in the center with wire, twisting tightly to puff it out. Make another one the same size and attach them to the flower stems with wire.

LE JARDIN

The selection of wrapping paper in the stores is just terrific. You will have a hard time deciding which one to use, because all the new French wired ribbons are just beautiful.

MATERIALS NEEDED

Beautiful floral paper
3 yards French wired ribbon

INSTRUCTIONS

1. Carefully wrap your box using the hints on page 24.

2. Wrap the ribbon around your package by starting in the front as shown in the illustration, then across the width of the box, and around the back up to the center-front. Twist here and continue to wrap the ribbon around your box lengthwise. Continue around to the center-front and tie in a knot leaving the ends about 8" long. This allows a smooth finish to the back of the box since the twist in the ribbon is under the knot on the front.

Illustration

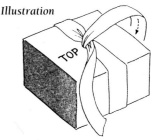

3. Make the bow, following the instructions on page 70 for the basic bow. This bow has 3 loops on each side about 3" long. Cut the tail end slightly longer than the loops. Attach the bow by using the tie ends on the package. Cut all ends on the diagonal. The French wired ribbon has tiny wires along each side and allows you creative freedom to bend and twist it into any shape you like. You will also love all the wonderful colors! This ribbon can be used over and over again.

FEMININE SPECIALTY WRAP

When looking for something unusual to add to a package, you may not have to look farther than your own backyard! **Marsha Ifland's** own garden flowers make beautiful bouquets as well as stunning package decorations.

Look at the magnificent effect you can get with wonderful french wired ribbon. The stores offer such a variety of colors and sizes —pick something that complements your paper and you'll have a gorgeous package!

A TOUCH OF LACE
• • • • • • • • • • • •

A touch of lace is so femi-nine. But lace roses, now that's extra special! This package was wrapped in a solid color shiny paper to enhance the lace. I found the lace on a spool in the ribbon section. This look is terrific!

MATERIALS NEEDED

Solid color wrapping paper
2 ¹/₂ yards of 4" wide lace
1 yard of artificial rope pearls

INSTRUCTIONS

1. After wrapping your package in a wonderful colored paper, tie a length of lace around your box with a simple knot in the center-front leaving the tie ends long. We used a 2 yard length of lace for the box pictured. Rather than cutting the ends on the diagonal, cut around the pattern of the lace to give the ends a classic look.

2. There are three roses on this box. To make the large rose...cut a 12" length of the lace down the middle lengthwise. Take one of these 2" x 12" strips and tightly roll one end three turns to form the center of your flower. Now gather the rest of the strip in your fingers around this center. Gradually turn as you gather to form your rose. See illustration #1. You can make your rose as open or as closed as you like by how tightly you gather the lace. Hold your rose in place with thin wire, twisted tightly, leaving the ends about 4" long to wire to the pack-age. To form the lace rose buds, use the remaining 12" strip of lace and cut in half to form 2 strips, each 2" x 6". Take one of these 6" long strips and tightly roll one end three turns to form the center of your rose bud. Now continue to roll the remaining lace loosely around this center to complete the rose bud. Wrap with wire as you did the large rose. Re-peat this process for the second rose bud.

Illustration #1

3. Wire the large rose and the two buds together and wire to your package over the lace knot. To hide the wire on the bottom of the roses, fold up one tie end of lace and wrap the underside with wire. Fold the tie end down over the wire. See illustration #2.

Illustration #2

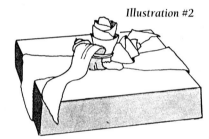

4. With wire, attach a 1 yard length of rope peals in loops under the roses. That adds the final elegant touch!

PRETTY PETALS
• • • • • • • • • • • •

Floral fabric is a wonder-ful way of customizing your gifts to look as if they were hand painted! This technique is fun and easy.

MATERIALS NEEDED

A solid color box
¹/₄ to ¹/₂ yard of floral fabric
(depends on the size of the flowers)
1 jar of decoupage coating
6 yards of ribbon
One silk flower

INSTRUCTIONS

1. Choose one of the beautiful flo-ral print fabrics available, and cut out the flowers and leaves. Arrange in an attractive pattern on your box. (Don't forget the sides of the box.) After you have decided where each flower should be placed, spread decoupage coating on the front and back of one fabric piece at a time and place it down on the box. Smooth out the air bubbles and wrinkles. Let it dry.

2. Tie a ribbon around your gift and make a grand bow, following in-structions on page 70. **HINT:** you can rent a bow making machine from an industrial supply store and make up bows to have on hand like the one shown in the photo.

3. Tuck in a beautiful silk flower that is color coordinated, and the look is complete. This box can be used over and over again for gifts, or to use as a jewelry box!

FEMININE SPECIALTY WRAP

The elegant look shown here is a result of solid color contrasting with soft, lace ribbon... spotlighting the beautiful lace roses, of course, you can make this work with any colors you pick. It's easy, effective and very feminine.

*Whenever a feminine look is desired, **Marsha Allen** emphasizes florals. Here, she started with a solid colored box and created her own "hand-painted" look. Not only was it fun to do, but just look at the professional results!*

SIMPLE ELEGANCE

. . . .

What a wonderful look you achieve when you use the natural open weave woven ribbon and the acetate moire together. I chose a wrapping paper with a design of twig hearts to go with the feeling of the natural woven ribbon.

MATERIALS NEEDED

Wrapping paper with a design of natural materials
6 yards of natural open weave ribbon
6 yards of acetate moire the same width as the woven ribbon

INSTRUCTIONS

1. After your box is wrapped following the instructions on page 24, place the natural open weave ribbon on top of the acetate moire ribbon and work with them together. Since the two ribbons together will have a heavy texture, you will want to wrap the box around lengthwise and overlap the ribbons slightly in the back. Cut and tape them to the box or staple them together. Now wrap the ribbons around the box from side to side and tie in the front, leaving the ends long.

2. Make a florist's bow with 3 loops on each side about 5" long. Cut the tail ends even with the end of the loops. Hold securely by twisting the wire. Tie the bow to the package with ribbon cut 20" long. Place the tie ribbon through the small center loop on the bow and around the center knot on the box. Tie securely under the bow. Pull the tie ends down and cut in a V shape to finish off. What a unique look!

HOME SWEET HOME

. . . .

Your gift doesn't have to be conventional. Look at this masterpiece created with a little imagination... and since these miniatures are available in most craft stores, bringing your own ideas to life will be a cinch!

MATERIALS NEEDED

Floral wrapping paper
Wicker furniture
Doily for rug
Miniature plant and votive candle glass
Tiny tea set

INSTRUCTIONS

1. Wrap your gift in beautiful floral paper, then place the darling wicker furniture on top. The square doily resembles a rug, and the miniature plant in a votive candle glass adds a touch of elegance as well as a living gift. The tiny tea set is a show of hospitality.

2. All the items are hot glued in place so nothing can slide off. These items can all be purchased at your craft store. Use your own creativity in decorating your gift box!

FEMININE SPECIALTY WRAP

Combining textures is the secret to this package's look. I experimented with using a woven ribbon right along with an acetate moire one. Don't be afraid to try unusual combinations like this — they really work!

Marsha Allen goes all out to celebrate a friend's new home. It's not as complicated as it looks, she assures us, and what an original way to celebrate!

CELEBRATION
. . . .

Too often beautiful bows are just thrown away. Why not try an original idea and make the bow an elegant gift in itself? With a few silk flowers and other craft store accessories, you can dress up a package in no time!

MATERIALS NEEDED

*Solid color paper
with a sheen
Small amount of a companion
paper
3 tiny sprigs of eucalyptus
a few clusters of dried baby's
breath
2 silk roses
1 corsage pin
2 ½ yards of ½" wide ribbon*

INSTRUCTIONS

1. Wrap your box in the solid color paper and trim with the matching print paper, glued in place.

2. The corsage is made by first arranging three tiny sprigs of eucalyptus, then a few clusters of dried baby's breath, and finally two silk roses. Secure together with hot glue and wire. Make the florist's bow following instructions on page 70 with 10 loops on each side, about 3" long. Cut the tail ribbon even with the loops. Tie the bow with a 10" length of ribbon. Attach the bow to the corsage stems over the spot where you put the hot glue. Stick a pearl headed corsage pin into the side of the corsage. Tape the corsage to the center of the box. Beautiful!

INNER BEAUTY
. . . .

How great your gift wrap will look inside the box. This adds that extra touch that turns something ordinary into something beautiful.

MATERIALS NEEDED

*Tissue paper (look for all the terrific new choices available)
Small amount of potpourri or confetti*

INSTRUCTIONS

1. Lay the tissue flat on the table and "walk" your fingers up each end, gathering the tissue as you go. Hold firmly in fingers. See illustration #1.

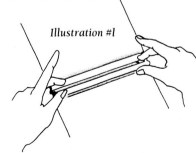

Illustration #1

2. Place the tissue in the bottom of the box. Arrange the gathers evenly.

3. Now for the element of surprise....sprinkle some fragrant potpourri or confetti throughout the gathers.

What a terrific look!

FEMININE SPECIALTY WRAP

*D*oni Linebarger presents her gift with an extra special touch. The corsage on the top of the box is ready to wear for the festive occasion.

*N*ot many gift-givers take the time to decorate even the inside of a box. Here, **Marsha Ifland** shows us just how effective this idea can be. Not only is it visually delightful, but the potpourri adds a rich aroma to absolutely any gift.

CLASSIC

Any man would feel extra special if he received a gift so elegantly wrapped in this dramatic gold and black!

MATERIALS NEEDED

Gold moire foil wrapping paper 4 yards of black and gold ribbon (the one I used has gold marbleizing over the black)

INSTRUCTIONS

1. Wrap your package carefully when using a foil paper, as it wrinkles easily. (See illustration on page 24.)

2. Wrap the ribbon around the box and tie a knot in the center. Leave the ribbon ends about 6" long.

3. Make a florist's bow following the instructions on page 70 with 5 loops on each side about 3 1/2" long. Cut the tail end 9 1/2" long. Tie the bow with a 14" length of ribbon, pulling it through the small center loop and under the knot on the package. Pull all the ribbon ends out and cut in a V shape.

Impressive!

SHIRTS-N-TIES

What fun you will have wrapping your gifts to resemble a shirt and tie! You can also get a great look with paper ribbon.

Checkered Shirt

MATERIALS NEEDED
*Bold wrapping paper
1 3/4 yards of 2" wide ribbon
1 pearl head corsage pin*

INSTRUCTIONS

1. Wrap your box in bold paper. This check looks great or you could use a stripe.

2. Tie a length of ribbon across your box near the top with the knot in the back.

3. Cut a length of ribbon about 27" long for the tie. (The length will vary depending on the size of your box.) Push the two cut ends of the ribbon underneath the front center point of the ribbon on the box. See illustration #1.

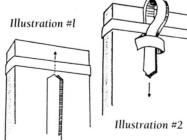

Illustration #1

Illustration #2

4. Pull the two cut ends of ribbon up over the top of the ribbon on the box and down through the loop...pull until the knot is formed for the tie. See illustration #2.

5. To make the tie tack, cut off a corsage pin leaving a 3/4" pin end.

Stick that through the center of the tie and into the box to hold in place. What a terrific look!

Striped Shirt
MATERIALS NEEDED

*White stripe wrapping paper
Small amount of marbleized, paisley or solid color paper for the tie
Two small buttons for the collar*

INSTRUCTIONS

1. Wrap the box with the pattern on your paper going up and down. Fold the paper in half to cut the collar so it has a double thickness. (The pattern on the paper should be going across for the collar.) Glue between the paper so it won't come apart. See illustration #1.

Illustration #1

2. Glue the collar in place (Note: Don't glue down the center of the collar until the tie has been put in place).

continued on page 72

MASCULINE SPECIALTY WRAP

Creating drama isn't difficult. It just takes some originality and imagination. Subtly patterned paper mixed with heavily textured ribbon is the key to this package's success.

*The smart looking red tie box was created by **Carley Watson**, and **Linda Lawrence** did a wonderful job creating the shirt-and-tie look shown here... the perfect solution for men of all ages. Linda also achieved a masculine look with paper ribbon.*

TUXEDO BOX
. . . .

Add an extra touch of class with a "no-frills" look to the gift for that very special man. Whether it's holiday time, a birthday party, or just a quiet evening, this wrap will get rave reviews.

MATERIALS NEEDED

Wrapping paper without a definite pattern
1 yard of ribbon (your choice)

INSTRUCTIONS

1. To determine where your pleats will begin, place the paper on the box and measure a third of the way in from the left edge, allowing plenty of extra paper for side flaps. Five pleats require approximately 7" so plan accordingly.

2. At this starting point make your first pleat (see illustration #1) and continue until five pleats have been completed

3. To secure pleating, apply a long strip of transparent tape at each edge of the paper (this will be hidden in back of box when done).

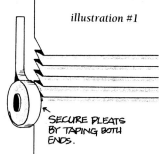
illustration #1

SECURE PLEATS BY TAPING BOTH ENDS.

4. Now you've prepared your paper for wrapping your package in the normal way! Be sure your taped edges create a seam on the back of the box.

5. For a finishing touch, tie a ribbon with a simple knot around the package if desired. This box will get rave reviews!!

TRADITIONAL
. . . .

Ribbons don't have to be made into bows to be effective. Here's what can be done by creating a "necktie" look with companion ribbons. The result is simple, classic and masculine.

MATERIALS NEEDED

Solid color wrapping paper (choose a rich color)
2 yards each of three companion ribbons

INSTRUCTIONS

1. After wrapping your box, place the center ribbon over the front and bring the end around to the back. Twist the ribbon and bring the ends around to the front and tie in a knot. Do this for each ribbon, feeding under the ribbon tied on the front. Space the ribbons about 1" apart.

2. The final touch is to tie the knot in a special way. Pull the ribbon ends on the knots down on the bottom and up on the top. Take the top ribbon end and wrap it around the tied ribbon just above the knot. See illustration #1.

Illustration #1

3. Now pull the end down through the loop you have just formed and line the ends up together. (See illustration #2.) Repeat for each ribbon.

Illustration #2

What a great traditional look for a man!

MASCULINE SPECIALTY WRAP

*L*eave it to **Marsha Ifland** to come up with a great look using wrapping paper and a few pleats! This cummerbund likeness really does "dress up" a package! Try it in black for added drama.

*W*hat a great time I had at the ribbon store picking out these beautiful companion ribbons. When my husband saw the completed package he said, "I would really feel special if I received a present wrapped like that!"

HIGH STYLE

. . . .

Creating unusual looks can be simple. Jazz up your packages by using ordinary contact paper! Complemented with the right ribbons, it all comes together —you'll be amazed at what you can create!

MATERIALS NEEDED

Contact paper
Ribbon-4 yards of each of the two colors for the large box and 2 yards of each of the two colors for the small ones

INSTRUCTIONS

1. Wrap your box following the hints on page 24. When you use contact paper, do not peel off the backing.

2. Tie the ribbons around the box following instructions on page 70, beginning in the front so you can avoid the twist in the back.

3. The bows were made with 8 loops, 3 ½" long for the large box and 6 loops 2 ½" long for the smaller boxes. Cut the tail ribbons even with the end of the loops. Tie the bow on to the package with a length of ribbon cut any length you desire. (Follow hints for bows on page 70.) Combining the marble look with the silver and black ribbon is stunning!

BRIGHT 'N BOLD

. . . .

Who wouldn't "brighten up" if they received a package wrapped in these terrific colors? The brighter the better if you want to lift someone's spirits.

MATERIALS NEEDED
Bright metallic paper
3 yards of metallic twist ribbon
1 yard of quick pompom
(just push up along the ribbon to gather)

INSTRUCTIONS
1. Wrap your package carefully when using foil paper as it will wrinkle easily.
2. Untwist the metallic twist ribbon and wrap around your package, tying with a knot in the front. Leave the tail ends 8" long.

3. Cut a length of untwisted ribbon 21" long and tie it around the knot in the center.
4. I hope you have found the quick pompom. They really add a great touch to your package. (Just push up on the ribbon to gather into a pompom and tie on over the center knot.)
5. Cut one more piece of untwisted ribbon 8 ½" long and tape under the knot so that there are 5 ribbon ends. Cut all ends on the diagonal. What a "bright spot" in someone's day.

MASCULINE SPECIALTY WRAP

*T*alented **Sandy Frye** wraps her gifts in a contemporary style for the men in her life! Would you believe that she used contact paper for these elegant wraps!

*N*ever underestimate the dazzling effect foil papers can have! They're dressy, festive and fun all at the same time. So make a gift-giving statement and brighten up someone's day.

ADORABLE CRITTERS

. . . .

Create a menagerie of lovable animal packages! Imagine how delighted a collector of dogs, kitties or pigs would be to receive one of these! They're simple to make and guaranteed to win hearts.

MATERIALS NEEDED

Wrapping paper that suits the type of animal you want to make.

INSTRUCTIONS

1. Wrap your box following instructions on page 24.

2. Cut the face and tails from the reverse side of the wrapping paper following any animal pattern you desire (coloring books are a great source).

3. The pig shown here has a 3-D look since the nose and feet are attached by a loop of paper on back, allowing them to stand out from the box surface. The ears have been cut separately and glued to the back of the head, tips rolled over and glued to the front. The tail holds its curly shape with wire taped to the inside, then curled around a pencil.

4. See photo for face cut-out of cat and dog. What child wouldn't love to have these little critters holding a special gift for them?!

JUNGLE BOX

. . . .

Just find any large print wrapping paper and cut out the design to create a sensational gift wrap!.

MATERIALS NEEDED

*Wrapping paper with a large design
Popsicle sticks*

INSTRUCTIONS

1. Wrap the box with the wrapping paper that has the design you like, or a solid color paper.

2. Cut out the designs you want to feature, and work out your arrangement on the box.

3. If the cut-out paper design will extend past the box, glue popsicle sticks to the back of the paper design so it won't flop over. Glue and tape your designs in place making sure the popsicle sticks are down past the top of the box so they hold rigidly in place.

4. The giraffe that you see next to the box is there for the photo purposes and when you design your box he would be taped to the top with your card in his mouth.

CHILDREN'S SPECIALTY WRAP

See what **Sylvia Eckhardt** has created! Sylvia collects pigs so naturally she made one for us to enjoy. The dog and kitty are adorable too!

Don't you love the way **Marsha Allen** has the lion peeking over the back and the alligator swimming off the box? The giraffe is holding the Birthday card in his mouth. We propped him up so you could see him. You can tape him to the top of your box.

COLOR ME HAPPY

. . . .

Stock up on small toys so you will have things on hand to decorate your gifts and make them unique.

MATERIALS NEEDED

Colorful wrapping paper
Curling ribbon
Small coloring book
Box of crayons

INSTRUCTIONS

1. Wrap your box in the colorful paper and tie the curling ribbon around twice each way, knotting in the front.

2. Curl the ribbon by running it over the sharp scissors blade and tie it on in a cluster over the knot on the box.

3. Add three extra long ribbons under the center cluster. Tie crayons to the ends of these ribbons, and tuck in a box of crayons and a coloring book under the cluster on the box!

CUT UPS

. . . .

A bright paper bursting with color that has a small size pattern is all you need to decorate a delightful gift box.

MATERIALS NEEDED

Colorful wrapping paper
with a small design
Bright ribbon
Glue

INSTRUCTIONS

1. Wrap your package, setting aside a few scraps of paper.

2. Tie the ribbon around the box with the knot in the front. Make a bow with three loops on each side about 3" long, cut tail end even with the loops. Tie the bow onto the package with a length of ribbon cut 14". (See bow instructions on page 70)

3. Cut out the designs you want to highlight from the scraps of wrapping paper. Glue the cutouts to the end of the loops on the bow. Super!

CHILDREN'S SPECIALTY WRAP

*K*ids love presents! But presents on top of presents . . . now that's original. **Linda Lawrence** shows us how to tantalize a youngster with this crayon theme, but you might try it with any number of small toys or party favors.

*C*lever **Julie Klinsky** has an easy way to make your packages unique! Cut out the bright colorful pattern from your gift wrap and use it on the bow for a new twist!

OUTSTANDING

How easy it is to make your gift look special! There are so many great wrapping papers available in the stores that you will have a wonderful time selecting just the right one for you. Look for wrapping paper that has a striking pattern, you can cut out for a "pop-up" effect.

MATERIALS NEEDED

Bright wrapping paper with a design that can be cut out easily
3x5 cards or old Birthday or Christmas cards

INSTRUCTIONS

1. After you have wrapped the box, decide what part of the design you want to "pop-up" and cut that out of a paper scrap.

2. Cut a 3x5 card (or old gift card) in a strip to cover the back of your design, plus an extra 1" on the bottom.

3. Glue the card strip to the back of the design and fold back the extra 1" on the bottom to create a flap to attach to package (see illustration #1).

Illustration #1

4. Place the "pop-up" cut out over the same design on the front of the box. Secure in place by putting glue on the underside of the flap and pressing on to the box (see illustration #2).

Illustration #2

You can add as many "pop-ups" as you like for a sensational package.

CITY STREETS

What a clever idea to turn the top of your gift into a city street bustling with tiny cars. This is fun and easy to do!

MATERIALS NEEDED

Colorful wrapping paper
3 to 4 yards of ½" wide ribbon
½ yard of ¼" wide ribbon
6 or 7 miniature cars
Hot glue

INSTRUCTIONS

1. Wrap the box in colorful paper.

2. Place one long strip of ½" wide ribbon for each outside line of the road around the box and tape on the back. You might need a few drops of glue on the front to hold the ribbons in place. It will be necessary to cross over the ribbons for the second road (see photo).

3. Cut the ¼" wide ribbon into 1" long strips and glue or tape in place for the center lines on the roads (see photo).

4. Attach the miniature cars and trucks with a bead of hot glue on one of the wheels.

5. Place a ready-made bow in the center if you like.

Great fun!

CHILDREN'S SPECIALTY WRAP

*Y*our gifts can appear elaborate with just the tiniest bit of ingenuity. Here's a way to bring attention to regular store-bought paper in a most unusual way. Kids love it!

*W*hat young boy wouldn't light up when he saw this delightful gift box by **Marsha Allen**? Isn't it amazing how simply she has converted an otherwise regular package surface into a miniature roadway?

BUILDING BLOCKS

. . . .

Now this is a clever idea! These building blocks will even add to the decor on the party table.

MATERIALS NEEDED

*Small square boxes
found in any
gift wrap section
Shiny letters and numbers in
primary colors
(these are found
in party stores
for making banners)
Glue
Mylar ribbon*

INSTRUCTIONS

1. Glue the letters and numbers to the sides of the boxes (or you could paint them on if you like).

2. Stuff the boxes full of treats and stack on top of each other.

3. Tie with shiny mylar ribbon to hold them all together as shown in the photo.

Adorable!

RAZZLE DAZZLE

. . . .

You can create a smashing gift wrap simply by using a dash of vibrant color.

MATERIALS NEEDED

*Wrapping paper
of your choice
Ribbon
Shredded mylar strips
(these come in
a package)*

INSTRUCTIONS

1. Wrap your box and tie with ribbon knotting in the front. Leave the ribbon ends about 10" long.
2. Place a handful of the shredded mylar over the knot on the package and tie the ribbon ends around them to secure.
Easy and dazzling!

CHILDREN'S SPECIALTY WRAP

$\mathcal{M}$arsha **Allen** has taken some simple items and put them together to come up with this great idea. These stacked blocks, chock-full of gifts, will delight any child and add a festive touch!

$\mathcal{C}$lever **Regina Benn** has put together a dazzling box simply by using shiny shredded mylar strips. The vibrant colors give an exciting touch!

WEDDING DAY
· · · · · · · · · · · ·

Wedding day, a most important event. Not all ceremonies are formal, but certainly formal wrap is appropriate. Be sure your gift reflects the mood of the occasion.

MATERIALS NEEDED

*Gold foil moire or elegant white wrapping paper
5 yards each of
three companion ribbons
(the large package has
gold lamé
and floral print lamé ribbons
and gold cording;
the smaller box has gold lamé,
white and gold taffeta
and white sheer fancy ribbons)*

INSTRUCTIONS

1. Wrap your box very carefully when using a foil paper as it will show wrinkles.

2. Tie all three ribbons around your box with the knots in the center front. Leave the tie ends about 12" long.

3. Make a bow, following instructions on page 70. This bow has 4 loops of each ribbon on either side. The loops are approximately 5" long. Cut the tail ribbons 12" long. Wire securely. (**HINT:** It is easier to work with no more than two ribbons together. Place one on top of the other and make your bow as usual. Add the third ribbon later.)

4. Tie the bow in place over the center knot on package with a 24" length of the third type of ribbon. Now make a bow from the third ribbon the same size as the others and tie it on to the center of the attached bow. When using cording, it works best to loop it back and forth rather than twisting as you did for a bow.

Note: Size your bow and length of the tie ends to your box! The sizes listed are for large packages. I know you will enjoy these wonderful ribbons. They can be used many times over for continued enjoyment.

(You might want to put one on a wreath for your door!)

WRAPPING HINTS

1. To determine the size of paper needed, place the box on the paper and pull it up around the box, adding an extra inch for overlap. Measure the length needed by pulling the paper up the sides from end to end. Mark your measurement and cut the paper to fit. Another way to determine how much paper you will need is to loop ribbon around the box, then lay the ribbon on the paper so you'll know where to cut.

2. Place the paper wrong side up and put your box in the center with the topside down. Bring the paper tightly around the box and overlap the ends. Use double-sided tape or transparent tape to hold securely.

3. Fold the paper down over the end of the box (trim off the excess). Miter the corners (see illustration #1) and fold the extending flap up and tape (see illustration #2).

Illustration #1   *Illustration #2*

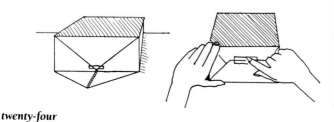

4. Another way to fold the ends is to fold both sides in towards the center to form two flaps. Sharply crease and miter the corners (see illustration #3). Fold one flap down and the other flap up, tape to hold (see illustration #4).

illustration #3

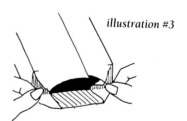

illustration #4

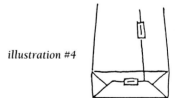

5. Turn the box over and run your fingers all around the edges of the box to give a finished look with sharp creases.

You can use a box over and over if you wrap the lid and box separately. It's easy, just follow these steps. . . .

continued on page 71

BEST WISHES
. . . .

The Bride and Groom will be delighted as you present to them a gift wrapped with tender loving care.

Silver and Net Box

MATERIALS NEEDED
Silver foil moire wrapping paper 5 yards of 5" wide net Silk white flower ornament with pearls for the top

INSTRUCTIONS

1. Carefully wrap the box in silver foil paper, watching for wrinkles.

2. Tie the net around the package with the knot on the center front, leaving the tie ends about 8" long.

3. Make a bow with the net, following instructions on page 70. This bow has 5 loops on each side about 5" long. Wire securely and tie onto the package over the center knot.

4. Wire on the silk flower ornament. Beautiful!

Metallic Ribbon Box
MATERIALS NEEDED
Silver foil moire wrapping paper 1 1/2 yards of sheer metallic fancy ribbon (you will need more if you have a large package) 10" of star garland

INSTRUCTIONS

1. After wrapping the box in a great paper, wrap the ribbon around with a simple tie bow on top. The ribbon used is a beautiful silver sheer with threads of gold running through.

2. Place a 10" length of star garland under the ribbons in the center of the box. Bring both ends up and over the bow and twist the wire to hold in place. Twist and curl the garland any way you like.

Gold Ribbon Box
MATERIALS NEEDED

White on white pattern paper any ribbon scraps

INSTRUCTIONS

1. After wrapping the box tie it with gold and white curling ribbon.

2. To tie as shown in the photo... begin on the top front left corner of the box and wrap the ribbon around the corner and down under the back right corner then up and over the corner on the bottom front. Continue the ribbon down and under the back left corner and up to tie together at the starting point. See illustration #1.

Illustration #1

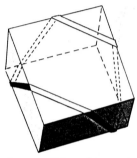

3. Curl some of the white and gold ribbon by running it across a scissor blade and tie on to the package. I made loops from two different ribbon scraps and tied them on.

4. The final touch was the ribbon rose. It was made from a scrap of 2 1/2" wide lamé ribbon about 12" long. Begin by tightly rolling one end two turns to form the center, then gently gather the rest of the ribbon in your fingers around this center. Gradually turn as you go until reaching the end of the ribbon. Hold the rose together with thin wire, twisted tightly. Wire on to the package for a wonderful look!

BASKET OF FLOWERS
. . . .

What bride wouldn't love to receive a gift like this in her favorite colors!

MATERIALS NEEDED

Large basket with handle Enamel spray paint 1/4- 1/2 yard of large floral print fabric (Note: amount depends on the print) 1/2 yard companion fabric print for bow 1 jar of découpage coating Gift of your choice to tuck inside

INSTRUCTIONS

See page 41 as the instructions for making this basket are the same as those for MARSHA's daughter's basket. They worked on these together as a Mother-Daughter project. They had a wonderful time and the results were fantastic!

WEDDING WRAP

*C*reative **Linda Lawrence** has found a wonderful look with netting.

    Regina Benn has created the adorable tiny silver box with a dusting of stars. The white box with a gold ribbon rose is elegant and easy to make from scraps of ribbon.

*C*lever **Marsha Allen** often presents her gift as two gifts in one...the basket itself and the item inside. The flowers on the basket are cut from fabric and the striped bow is also fabric... easy to do!

FROM THE HEART
· · · · · · · ·

Say "I Love You" with a tenderly wrapped gift. These designs will win the heart of that special person. **Linda Lawrence** found a wonderful Victorian print paper for her package and tied it with delicate feather edge satin ribbon.

I found the wonderful French wired ribbon in a lamé floral print and it made a spectacular bow! And look at the great touch with shiny iridescents on the little pink box!

Victorian Box
MATERIALS NEEDED

Sweet Victorian wrapping paper
3 yards of ¹/₂" wide feather edge satin ribbon
Gold heart sticker

INSTRUCTIONS

1. Wrap your box following hints on page 24 and tie with ribbon.

2. Make the bow as per instructions on page 70. This bow has 6 loops on each side about 2 ¹/₂" long. Cut the tail end even with loops. Wire to secure.

3. Tie the bow to the package with a length of ribbon cut 8" long. Pull ends down and cut on the diagonal. Place a heart sticker on the ribbon end for a tender touch.

Wired Ribbon Box
MATERIALS NEEDED

Shiny wrapping paper in a wonderful solid color
5 ¹/₂ - 6 yards of French wired ribbon in lamé floral print

INSTRUCTIONS

1. After wrapping your package, tie the ribbon, beginning on the front and going around the side and up to the beginning point, twist and continue in the opposite direction. Pull ribbon all the way around to the beginning point on the front of the box and tie in a knot. Be sure to leave the tie ends about 10" long.

2. Make your bow with 4 loops on each side about 5" long following instructions on page 70. Cut the tail ribbon even with the loops.

3. Tie the bow to the package with a length of ribbon cut 24" - 28" long. Cut all tie ends on the diagonal.

4. Curl two of the tie ends around a pencil and gently pull to slightly loosen. Bend two other ends into a pleasing shape. That's the beauty of wired ribbon... you can put it in any shape you like and it will hold! Pull out the bow loops, and you have a dazzling gift presentation. You will enjoy this ribbon as it can be used over and over again!

Tiny Pink Box
MATERIALS NEEDED

Beautiful wrapping paper
6 yards of ribbon
Shredded iridescents
(these are sold in a package)

INSTRUCTIONS

1. Wrap your box with beautiful paper and tie with ribbon, knotting in the center.

2. The bow on this box is a pompom bow, see instructions on page 71

3. Place a cluster of glimmering shredded iridescents on top of the knot on the box and tie the bow on top. What a sweet look!

EASTER BUNNIES

You won't be able to resist these adorable bunnies! They can hold your special Easter gift or be used to hold goodies on an Easter egg hunt. Make them for a girl or boy by adding a bow or leaving plain. These cuties were made from lunch bags!

MATERIALS NEEDED

Regular size lunch bags in white, yellow or pink
Black felt tip pen
Pink squeeze bottle fabric paint (optional)
Stapler
Easter grass

INSTRUCTIONS

1. Pull out the side pleats on the lunch bag and cut out the bunny as shown in illustration.

Illustration

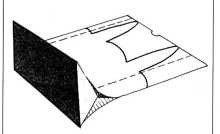

2. Draw the face and ears on bag as shown in the photo. Accent with pink squeeze bottle fabric paints, if you like, by making a pink nose and cheeks and squiggly lines on ears.

3. You can add a squeeze bottle fabric paint bow to the girl bunny if you like. For a nice touch, sprinkle glitter over nose, cheeks and bow while paint is still wet.

4. Staple the tips of the ears together to form a handle. The children can slip their arm through the side.

5. Fill with Easter grass. Hide your gift inside the grass. These bunnies would be great favors for a children's party as they are Fast, Fun, and Easy to make!

PINK NET PUFF & LAVENDER BOX

A touch of netting, flowers tucked under a bow, a dainty paper doily . . .all simple things. When added to a gift wrap, simple turns to sensational!

Pink Net Puff
MATERIALS NEEDED
Wrapping paper in small print
1 yard of net
3 ³/₄ yards each of
1¹/₂" and ¹/₂" wide ribbon
in contrasting colors
INSTRUCTIONS
1. Wrap your box in your choice of paper.
2. Fold the net in half and place the wrapped box in the middle. Pull the net up around the box and tie with ribbon on the center top to create the big puff. Leave the tie ends on the ribbon long to cascade down the front of the box. (Note: If you are using two different ribbons as shown in photo work with them together treating them as one.) Fan the net ends out over the box and pull up to create the look you want.
3. Make bow following instructions on page 70. This bow has 3 loops of each color on either side. Each loop is about 3 ¹/₂" long. Cut the tail ribbon even with the ends of the loops. Wire the bow to secure.

4. Cut a length of ribbon about 20" long for the tie. Push one end of this ribbon up under the knot on top of the package, pulling until the ends are equal in length. Tie the bow on with this ribbon, placing the knot under the bow.

5. Pull all the ribbon ends down and leave long. Cut the tip ends on the diagonal
Quick & Lovely!

Lavender Box
Wrap your gift in a shiny solid color paper and tie with iridescent tulle netting. Place a dainty paper doily under the knot and slip in a few sprigs of dried lavender that is tied with curling ribbon. Simple yet delightful!

*S*pring is here! Easter bunnies are definitely hopping about, so why not get in to the spirit? These irresistible little guys are so fast, fun, and easy to make, you may end up with a hutchfull!

*J*ust one yard of pink net is all it took to transform this package from looking ho-hum to terrific! And what could be more pleasant than to receive **Marsha Ifland's** lavender scented package?

CHRISTMAS MORNING

· · · · · · · · · · · · · ·

Oh how my family loves Christmas! My talented daughter, Julie McGaha, goes all out to make her gift packages special for her handsome husband and two adorable boys. This year she had fun wrapping all her gifts alike for a great look under the tree! Some of the packages she sent home to us are shown in the center of the photo, all tied with shiny gold ribbon.

I always wrap gifts my in coordinating companion papers and tie them all with Christmas red ribbon. Use different types of bows to complement the size of the box. Another idea might be to choose a ribbon color for each family member and wrap all the gifts for that person in the same color ribbon as the Royal family in England does.

MATERIALS NEEDED

Red foil moire wrapping paper
Shiny gold twisted foil ribbon
Red and gold shredded mylar strips (these come in a bag)
Gold star garland
Several rolls of coordinating companion wrapping paper
Large spool of red ribbon (1 ½" or 2" wide)
Transparent tape

INSTRUCTIONS

1. Wrap your packages in either the red foil moire paper or the coordinating Christmas wrap. (See wrapping hints on page 24.)

2. Untwist the gold foil twisted ribbon and wrap around the red foil boxes, tying on the center front. Tie the coordinated wrapped packages with red ribbon. Use different types of bows to complement the size of the box. (See bow instructions on page 70).

3. Place a few strands of red and gold shredded mylar strips and a 12" length of gold star garland on the top of the red foil packages. Tie the gold foil untwisted ribbon in a knot to hold everything in place. Curl the wired star garland around a pencil, then gently pull to loosen slightly, for a finished look!

May you and your loved ones have a very Merry Christmas!

HOLIDAY WRAP

We asked a group of young-
sters to actually do these
projects. We thought you
would like to know who
these terrific kids were.
Seated in the front row,
Elizabeth Neff, Matthew
Neff, Michael Klinsky.
Standing in the back row,
left to right, Andrew
Klinsky, Lynelle Allen,
Mike Hagen, Matt Hagen,
Katie Hagen, Annie
Klinsky, Courtney Slagel,
Robert Patterson, Richard
Patterson, Brandon
McGaha (Photo inset)
Fantastic results kids!

STICKER FUN

MATERIALS NEEDED
White craft paper
Colorful stickers
Color marking pens
Curling ribbon,
shredded iridescents or
craft ribbon

INSTRUCTIONS
1. Wrap your box with white craft paper.
2. Look over all your stickers and pick a theme for your sticker art. Draw your picture on the front of the box and place your stickers exactly where you want them. Finish off your art with colorful marking pens.
3. Finish your package with shiny curling ribbon as we did on the zoo box, or shredded iridescents that look great on the underwater box.

The car sticker box is decorated with red craft ribbon. Cut 7 strips of ribbon 6" long and tie together in the middle for each corner decoration. Fan out the ribbon strips for a nice effect.

SUMMERTIME

Yarn Box
MATERIALS NEEDED
White craft paper
Thick, colorful yarn scraps
Glue (clear drying)
INSTRUCTIONS
1. Wrap your box with white craft paper and draw your picture on the box in pencil.
2. Place a line of glue along your pencil lines, doing a small section at a time. Put the yarn over the glue and run your finger along, pressing on to the box. Continue until the drawing lines are completely covered with yarn.

Fabric Flower Box
MATERIALS NEEDED
White craft paper
Small scraps of colorful fabric
Glue
Colorful tape (optional)
Color marking pens

INSTRUCTIONS

1. Wrap your box with white craft paper.

2. Cut scraps of fabric into $1/2$" and $1 1/2$" circles.

3. Put a drop of hot glue in the center of the circle on the wrong side of the fabric. Pinch the fabric together in your fingers and hold for a second while the glue dries. (Be extra careful with hot glue since its easy to burn yourself.)

4. Place a drop of hot glue on the box where you want your flower garden. Press the side of your fabric flower onto the glue, holding for a second to secure. Continue until all

Continued on page 72

FUN FOR CHILDREN WRAP

*C*reate a gift wrap with stickers! **Annie Klinsky**, age 10, made a zoo scene. **Courtney Slagel**, age 9, chose underwater animals, and 7 year-old **Andrew Klinsky** made a city street scene.

*M*atthew Neff, age 6, created this fun snail and butterfly wrapping paper with yarn! The colorful flower meadow wrap was made with fabric scraps by **Annie Klinsky**, age 10. They are adorable!

BLOW ART

Food coloring, a straw, and white craft paper is all it takes to create wonderful wrapping paper! All the children wanted to work on this project because it was so much fun, and they liked the results of their work.

MATERIALS NEEDED

Several colors of food coloring
White craft paper
Straw
Fine glitter (optional)
Polypropylene, print, shiny or satin ribbon

INSTRUCTIONS

1. Cut the white paper to the size needed to wrap your box and tape the corners to the table. (Be sure the table surface is washable.)

2. Drop a dot of food coloring anywhere you want on your paper and gently blow on it through the straw. This creates interesting patterns of color. When one color is dry, repeat with another color to achieve a spectacular look.

3. Wrap your package after your design is completely dry. You can sprinkle on a hint of fine glitter if you like (spray the paper with glue to hold the glitter in place.)

4. Tie your gift with ribbons that enhance the colors in your art (see bow instructions on page 70.) We used a shiny red ribbon to enhance the touch of glitter on the design. The yellow ribbon is polypropylene and we used a ribbon shredder on the ends. (See directions below under Spatter Painting for instructions.) There are so many adorable print ribbons to use on a child's gift. In fact, the ribbon selections are all fabulous!

SPATTER PAINTING!

Food coloring, a toothbrush and a stencil is all it takes to achieve these delightful packages. The kids had a great time with this fast . . . fun . . . and easy project. Shredded polypropylene ribbon adds the final exciting touch!

MATERIALS NEEDED

White craft paper
Food coloring
Stencils
Old toothbrush
One yard of each color of polypropylene ribbon
Ribbon shredder

INSTRUCTIONS

1. Cut your white paper to the size needed for the box, and tape the corners down on a washable surface.

2. Place the stencil on the paper so it will be on the front of the box when the package is wrapped. If you don't have a stencil, just cut any shape that you like from paper or a picture from a magazine.

3. Put the food coloring in a bowl. Dip in the old toothbrush then shake it over the bowl to remove excess drips. Use the brush medium dry.

4. Point the bristles down toward the paper and run your thumb across them to achieve the spatters. Continue this process until the color is as vibrant as you like.

5. Remove the stencil after it has dried and your shape is outlined on the paper. Wrap the package, being sure to place the pattern in the center.

Ribbon Shredder Instructions

If this is the first time you have used a ribbon shredder, you're in for a treat. You can shred any type of ribbon that splits lengthwise. Test the ribbon by trying to make a short tear on one end. If it tears easily, it will shred. We used a polypropylene ribbon in vibrant colors to enhance these packages. It took one yard of each color of ribbon. The little plastic ribbon shredder is inexpensive and you can do so many things with it. You will receive instructions when you purchase one, but basically the ribbon shreds as you pull it through the shredder teeth. Just begin shredding 1" from the end and continue to within 1" of the other end. Make a loop and tie it in the middle, and you have a brilliant burst of color to tie on your package.

FUN FOR CHILDREN WRAP

Elizabeth Neff age 3, designed the box tied in a lamb print ribbon, **Matthew Neff**, age 6, created the box on the left. **Annie Klinsky** age 10, designed the box with the shiny red bow. **Courtney Slagel**, age 9, created the box tied with yellow ribbon.

Katie Hagen, 12, chose a splash of red, and her 10-year-old brother, **Matt Hagen**, chose green food coloring to create a spatter color frame around their animal stencils. The shredded ribbon provides the perfect finishing touch.

DESIGNER PRINTS

Carve a bar of soap, or cut shapes from a tiny piece of foam rubber. . . add some paint and paper and you have the ingredients for a lot of fun and great wrapping paper!

MATERIALS NEEDED

Craft paper, brown mailing paper or brown paper bags
Small piece of foam rubber or bar of soap
Acrylic craft paints (tole, tempera...)
Ink pad
Twine or raffia for tying

INSTRUCTIONS

1. Wrap your box with either the white craft paper or brown bags.

2. Cut simple shapes from dense rubber. (You can use a coloring book for patterns if you like.) Or, if you're creative, carve any shape you like from a bar of soap.

3. Pour the acrylic paint into a pie plate. Wet the foam rubber and smear it around to cover the bottom surface with paint. If you are using the carved bar of soap, you will get the best results with an ink pad. Practice "stamping" on scrap paper before you begin on your box.

4. Plan out where you want the designs to go on the box and then "stamp" them on. Let dry. (Be sure to wash paint off foam so they can be used again.)

5. Ties from twine or raffia look great on these packages. The raffia is just looped over to create a bow.

6. Stamp an extra shape on a scrap piece and cut it out for the tag.
Fast...Fun...Easy

MY BEST FRIEND

Create a special wrap by simply using pictures of your favorite things cut from magazines. If you're decorating a gift for a grandparent, you could find pictures that remind you of the special things they do for you.

MATERIALS NEEDED

Several old magazines
Box with a sturdy lid
5 yards of ribbon
Scissors
Glue

INSTRUCTIONS

1. Carefully cut out your favorite pictures from old magazines.

2. Glue the pictures directly on the box lid rather than wrapping with paper, so the box can be used again to hold small treasures. Overlap the pictures slightly, and don't forget to decorate the sides of the box.

3. Tie your pretty package with a pom-pom bow. See the instructions on page 71. What fun to receive a gift wrapped like this!

FUN FOR CHILDREN WRAP

Michael Klinsky, age 4, stamped hearts on his box... **Andrew Klinsky**, age 7, likes pine trees. Their mom, **Julie Klinsky**, joined the fun and printed a star in the sky. **Robert Patterson**, age 11, carved a fantastic tree from a bar of soap!!

Twelve year-old **Katie Hagen** *loves animals, so naturally she chose pictures of adorable dogs to decorate her box. Just looking at this gift makes you smile!*

thirty-nine

FLOWER BASKET

. . . .

A decorated basket is a wonderful way to present your gift! The basket will be used again and again. This project takes a little extra time but it is well worth the effort!

MATERIALS NEEDED

Large basket with handle
Enamel spray paint
¹/₄-¹/₂ yard of large floral print fabric
(Note: amount depends on the print)
¹/₂ yard companion fabric for bow
1 jar decoupage coating
Gift of your choice to tuck inside

INSTRUCTIONS

1. Spray paint the basket or leave natural if you like.

2. Cut the floral designs out of fabric and decide where you want to place them on the basket. Be sure to decorate the sides of the basket.

3. Cover the front and back of the fabric flowers with decoupage coating following the instructions on the label. Place on the basket where desired. Use a blunt instrument like a pencil to tap the fabric into the weave on the basket to adhere better.

4. Bow instructions (the handle on the basket in photo is 8" across. It took a 2 yard long strip of fabric to make the bow so this can help you gauge the amount of fabric you will need.) Cut two strips of fabric each 6" long x 45" wide (or whatever the width of your fabric). By cutting across the width of the fabric, instead of lengthwise, you will save on fabric.

5. Place fabric strip on sink counter with the wrong side facing you. Fold each side in to meet in the center to give you a 3" wide strip of fabric.

6. Generously cover both sides of fabric with decoupage coating (it dries clear). Hang up until it is damp dry.

Continued on Page 72

IMAGINATION BONANZA

. . . .

Kids enjoy using squeeze bottle paints which come in a beautiful array of colors. We show you how to design a pattern for gift wrapping paper, and add extra interest with the paints. And what a lively note a dash of color adds to a plain lunch bag that is used to hold an unusually shaped gift.

MATERIALS NEEDED

White craft paper
Several colors of squeeze bottle fabric paint
3 x 5 card
Brown lunch bag
Shiny curling ribbon
craft ribbon

INSTRUCTIONS

1. Use the 3 x 5 card to make a pattern for your paper. Cut off the long edge of the card in a pattern of your liking. Tape the cut-off piece of card to the opposite edge of the card, matching the straight edge of the cut piece to the straight edge of the card. Repeat with the short edge of the card. (See illustration.)

Illustration

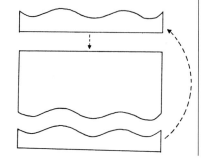

2. Trace the pattern you have created from the 3 x 5 card onto your paper . . . the pattern will fit together like a puzzle.

3. Outline your design in different colors of paints, and you can draw in the center of the design if the shape resembles an animal or whatever.

4. The lunch bag was colored with a sponge and different colored ink pads. Color the stripes onto the bag, or you can cut the sponge into a fun shape and print on the bag using the ink pads.

5. The lunch bag was tied with shiny curling ribbon for added interest. The more you use the better. The ribbon on the puff paint box is just tied on with a knot in the center front. Cut a length of ribbon 20" long and fold in half . . . place it over the knot and tie onto the package.

Delightful!

$\mathcal{S}$ee what **Lynelle Allen**, age 13, created with a basket, fabric and decoupage coating! She had a great time making this wonderful gift. It is fairly easy to do but it does take some time.

$\mathcal{E}$leven-year-old **Robert Patterson** shows us a clever way to design a pattern for wrapping paper. Seven-year-old **Mike Hagen** placed a dash of color on a simple brown lunch bag for a wonderful gift wrap.

FLURRY OF FLUORESCENCE

· · · · · · · · · ·

Cardboard rolls from paper towels, cookie cutters and a few other supplies are all it takes to help you design your own wrapping paper. Kids love the exciting fluorescence of color that the prints and ribbon add to their handiwork!

MATERIALS NEEDED

*White craft paper
Cardboard rolls from paper towels or bathroom tissue
Cookie cutters
Small amounts of. . .
embroiidery thread or
string and beads
Any kind of paint
Glue
Ribbon*

INSTRUCTIONS

Pink Lattice Work Design

1. Glue embroidery thread or string onto a cardboard roll from paper towels in a criss-cross pattern.

2. Roll the cardboard in the paints. (**HINT:** A thin layer of paint will give the best results.)

3. Roller print onto the white craft paper by holding your fingers at each end of the cardboard roll and go over the paper.

Orange and Yellow Design

1. Cut simple shapes in two cardboard rolls.

2. Roll one cardboard in the bright orange paint and go over your paper (see hints listed above). After it has dried, use the second cardboard and roll it in the bright yellow paint. Go over the orange print in the opposite direction. The shapes will not be a sharp image but will give the paper an interesting texture.

Bead Design

1. Glue beads of tiny sizes and shapes (we used half-moon shapes) to the cardboard roll.

2. Roll the cardboard in the paint and go over the paper

3. After the design has dried, you can outline some of the shapes with marking pens or paint so they stand out.

Cookie Cutter Design

1. Dip the cookie cutter in the paint and print the shape on the white craft paper. (**HINT:** This works best when you use thick paint.)

2. This project was so much fun that after the heart-shaped print was completed, the boys used duck-shaped cookie cutters to print paper for their Mom so she could wrap a baby gift.

HANDS ON

· · · · · · · · · ·

What grandparent wouldn't be thrilled to receive a package personalized with hand and fingerprints! All you need are ink pads and colored marking pens plus a childs imagination, and youre on your way to making a charming design.

MATERIALS NEEDED

*White craft paper
Ink pads
Colored marking pens
Ribbon
(use polypropylene if you are
using a ribbon shredder)*

INSTRUCTIONS

1. Wrap your box in white paper.

2. Decide on what your design will be. Press your finger on the ink pad and then onto the paper. (You can color fingers with a marking pen and print on the box.)

3. Fill in the details with colored pens. Let your imagination flow for your own designs!

4. We had fun with the ribbon shredder again! (See instructions on page 36.) The ribbon flower on Mike's hand box was done with two 6" scraps of polypropylene ribbon. Begin shredding 1" in from the end and continue within 1" of the other end. Make a loop with each ribbon. Hold the solid ends together and tie in the center to form the flower. See the illustration. Tape the flower to the corner of the box. We ran ribbon along the side of the box for a finished look.

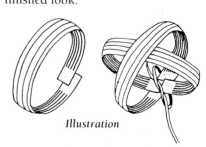

Illustration

FUN FOR CHILDREN WRAP

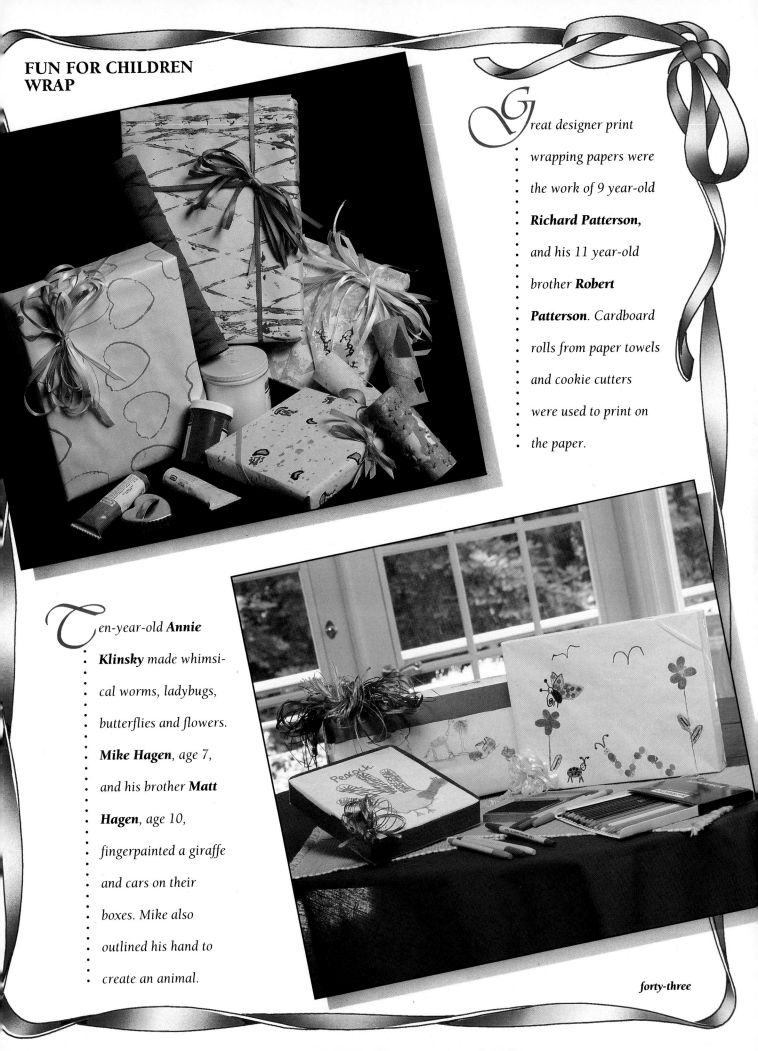

*G*reat designer print wrapping papers were the work of 9 year-old **Richard Patterson,** and his 11 year-old brother **Robert Patterson**. Cardboard rolls from paper towels and cookie cutters were used to print on the paper.

*T*en-year-old **Annie Klinsky** made whimsical worms, ladybugs, butterflies and flowers. **Mike Hagen**, age 7, and his brother **Matt Hagen**, age 10, fingerpainted a giraffe and cars on their boxes. Mike also outlined his hand to create an animal.

LITTLE ARTISTS

There is something warm and tender about art work from our little ones. Can't you just see the face of a three-year-old when someone he loves tells him how terrific his present looks! It's important to make time in your family for special moments like these!

MATERIALS NEEDED

Any child's art work
Glue or tape
Ribbon in colors to enhance the art

INSTRUCTIONS

1. Tape or glue the art work to the top of a sturdy box. (You could wrap the box in a bold solid color wrapping paper to highlight the art.)

2. We used three colors of ⅛" satin ribbon with lots of loops for the bow to give the finishing touch.

3. The tie is a great idea for Fathers Day, or to decorate a man's gift box anytime. Cut the tie out of bright construction paper. Cut tiny scraps of colorful paper and let your toddler glue them to the tie. The one in the photo was made at a preschool where the teacher glued a tiny pipe cleaner hook on the back and all the Daddies wore their ties (made with tender loving care) to church on Fathers Day.

BATTER UP

This is truly a fast . . . fun . . . and easy project! The kids will be able to decorate a gift box in no time at all with baseball cards! The cards are attached with a tiny piece of double-stick tape so they can be removed without damaging them.

MATERIALS NEEDED

Solid color wrapping paper or box
Selection of baseball cards
Polypropylene ribbon and ribbon shredder
Double-stick tape

INSTRUCTIONS

1. Wrap the box in a bold solid-colored wrapping paper.

2. Cut a tiny piece of double-stick tape and place it on the back of the card in the center. Arrange on the box as desired. (One card in the center of a small box looks great!)

3. The finishing touch on this package is polypropylene ribbon tied around the top and bottom. The tie ends are shredded with that wonderful ribbon shredder. (See instructions on page 36.)

FUN FOR CHILDREN WRAP

$\mathcal{U}$se your toddler's art to decorate your packages! My little three-year-old grandson, **Brandon McGaha**, sponge painted a whale, and glued tiny scraps of paper to the tie his preschool teacher had cut from construction paper.

$\mathcal{K}$ids and baseball cards go together! **Linda Lawrence** thought of this idea for her boys to decorate their gifts for friends.

RAGS TO RICHES

. . . .

Brown cardboard containers can be changed into something extraordinary! It's easy to do . . . just tie a knot in a rag, dip it in paint and dab onto the box. Add a little glitter accent and you have a wonderful gift box!

MATERIALS NEEDED

Brown cardboard box or plain gift box
Small amount of
2 or 3 shades of paint
Small rags
Glitter
Feather (optional)
Beautiful ribbons of your choice

INSTRUCTIONS

1. Tie a knot in the middle of a small rag.

2. Dip the knot in one of the darker colors of paint. (Sylvia used semi-gloss enamel and flat paint left over from another project. Use whatever you have on hand that is color coordinated.)

3. Hold each end of the rag and roll the knot across the box.

4. Let the first color dry, then dip the knotted rag in another color of paint and roll that across the box in the opposite direction. You can use the knot to dab paint on in spots if needed. Let some of the box show through for a marbling effect.

5. Sylvia added a third color to the larger box by dipping a feather in paint and lightly brushing some areas on the box. She then used spray glue and dusted a handful of glitter on the front for added pizzazz!

6. The final touch are these simply gorgeous ribbons! A French wired pleated lame ribbon tied in a huge bow makes a statement all its own! The gold lame ribbon is also wired and adds a simple elegant look! The beauty of this ribbon is that you can bend and twist it into any shape you like and the wire holds it in place . . plus you can use it over and over again!

Simply beautiful!

MADE FROM SCRAPS

. . . .

Save all the small pieces of paper and ribbon left over from other gift wrap to create your own original "one-of-a-kind" combinations. If you purchase papers and ribbons that are color-coordinated, you will have a nice selection of scraps for pairing together.

MATERIALS NEEDED

Any left over wrapping paper that is color coordinated
Ribbon
Glue

INSTRUCTIONS

Patchwork Wrap

1. Cut 4" x 5" squares of paper (Linda used different baby shower paper scraps).

2. Sew the paper together in a patchwork design using the zig-zag stitch on your machine. You could glue them together if you'd like.

3. The bow on this package has seven loops on each side about 3" long (see bow instructions on page 70).

Ribbon Scrap Wrap

Linda's small box was wrapped in gift paper then tied with ribbon with the knot on the front. Fold another scrap of ribbon in half and place over the knot, then tie on to secure. Cut all the ribbon ends on the diagonal.

Companion Papers

1. Used scraps from three different companion papers to create the variety shown in the photo.

2. Cut borders or other details from the pattern to glue on as you like.

3. Wrap the lids separately, as well as the bottoms of the box, so you can use them again and again (see how-to's on page 71).

4. Mix several different ribbon scraps together to make them go further. You can create fresh new looks each time!

CREATE-A-WRAP

an you believe a little
paint on a rag can
create this smashing
look! **Sylvia Eckhardt**
transformed plain
cardboard boxes into
something fabulous!

oni **Linebarger** and
Linda Lawrence never
throw away a scrap of
ribbon or wrapping
paper. Linda made up
the patchwork wrap
and also the middle
box using a small scrap
of ribbon. Doni used
scraps of companion
papers for her gifts.

COUNTRY GARDEN
· · · · · · · · · · ·

Collect flowers from your garden or the roadside and dry them hanging upside down in a dark place. You can also find a nice selection of dried flowers in the stores.

MATERIALS NEEDED

Small amounts of the following:
Tall pink and purple larkspur
White German statice
Purple statice and pepper grass
Caspia or latafolia
spanish moss, twigs,
One rosebud
any green leaf foilage
1 yard of ⅛" wide satin ribbon
Tiny bird

INSTRUCTIONS

1. Wrap the lid of a sturdy box with shiny white paper. (See how-to's on page 24.)

2. Hot glue a 2" wide strip of spanish moss all across the bottom of the box.

3. Hot glue tall stems of filler flower such as latafolia or caspia on the left side of the box, tucking the stems into the Spanish moss.

4. Glue in 2 or 3 tall stems of larkspur then more latafolia, pepper grass and statice as shown in the photo. The best look is achieved when you build your garden layer-upon-layer and the stems appear as if they are growing out of the Spanish moss.

5. To make the rustic fence...break twigs into 2" lengths for the posts and railings. Set the posts into the spanish moss and onto the lid with hot glue about 2" apart. This box has 5 fence posts beginning on the far right and extending just past the center of the box. Now place the twigs across the posts for the railings, one near the bottom and one near the top. (See photo.)

6. Glue in some latafolia, statice and flower heads from the larkspur on both sides of the fence to give dimension. Make the garden extra full on the left side, fewer flowers in the middle, and medium full on the right side. (See photo.)

7. Glue in some twigs, a rosebud and greens on the left side. Add twigs and greens on the right.

8. Glue a tiny bird on the top of the fence to watch over things in the garden.

9. Make a small bow from the satin ribbon with 3 loops on each side about 1 ½" long. (See bow instructions on page 70.) Tie the bow with a 8" length of ribbon. Glue the bow to the lower left side of the box. This box can sit on the dresser and hold jewelry or other treasures! This project will take more time than most, but it will be worth it!

SPATTER PAINT
· · · · · · · · · · ·

If you want a fresh new original gift wrapping paper, then this project is for you! A gentle tapping of the toothbrush that has been dipped in watercolor paint is all it takes to create this flurry of color.

MATERIALS NEEDED

White craft paper
Watercolors
Toothbrush
Ribbon

INSTRUCTIONS

1. Lay the paper flat and tape the corners down to prevent curling when wet.

2. Fill 3 jars with water and the watercolors of your choice. (You won't need much paint as it is very concentrated.) Fill a 4th jar with plain water.

3. Dip the toothbrush into the watercolors and hold over the paper, bristle-side down. Tap the toothbrush handle against your hand for the spatter effect, moving over the surface quickly and evenly. Very little movement is necessary for the larger drops.

4. Let the first color dry before going on to the next, making sure to rinse out the brush in plain water between applications. Continue spatter painting until you like the look.

5. Sandy wrapped her gift boxes and tied them with curling ribbon. She used 3 of the colors in the spatters for a great look.

CREATE-A-WRAP

*Y*ou can almost smell the flowers and hear the bird sing when you see this country garden box! Create your own garden complete with a country fence from dried flowers and twigs.

*C*reative **Sandy Frye** used watercolors and an old toothbrush to achieve this smashing gift wrap! It's fast . . . .fun . . . and easy to do!

WALLPAPER BOX/TOTE BAG

Leftover wallpaper from home decorating projects can make exciting gift wrap! You can also make a matching accessory for your dresser by wrapping the lid and bottom of a box separately and using it to hold jewelry.

Nosegay Box

MATERIALS NEEDED

Wallpaper
3 stems of white statice
3 artificial leaves
(paper, velvet or satin)
1 stem of wired cluster pearls
small amount green
florist's tape (optional)
1 ½ yards
¼" wide gold ribbon
5 yards 1" wide
ribbon wire

INSTRUCTIONS

1. Wrap box using wallpaper and tie with color coordinated 1" wide ribbon.

2. Wire together three stems of white statice.

3. Wire to the flower stems three artificial leaves placing one in the front center and one on each side. Wire the pearl stems to the front.

4. Begin wrapping the florist's tape under the leaves and extend down to stem ends.

5. Tie an 8" length of ¼" ribbon just under the leaves. Make a small bow with 3 loops on each side about 1 ½" long. (See bow instructions on page 70.) Attach the bow to the nosegay with the ribbon you attached under the leaves.

6. Make a bow using the 1" wide ribbon. This bow has 6 loops on each side about 1 ½" long. Cut the tail end even with the loops. Attach this bow to the package over the knot with a length of ribbon cut 10" long.

7. Attach nosegay to the center of bow on the package with wire.

continued on page 72

CINDERELLA FINISH

A plain tote bag in a pretty color and matching tissue is a great beginning for a fabulous wrap, especially for the large or unusual shaped gifts!

MATERIALS NEEDED

Plain colorful tote bags
Color coordinated tissue paper
Victorian or floral stickers
1 yard of silk cording
2 tassels in color to
match cording
2 cotton hand towels with
lace trim
3 yards of ⅛" satin ribbon
¾ yard of ½" ribbon
for handle

INSTRUCTIONS
Tote Bag

1. A Victorian rosebud heart was placed on the small bag and a large rose on the large bag. Rather than placing the sticker right in the middle, put it either to the right or left side on the top or bottom or in the center on the bottom.

2. Wrap your gift in a colorful tissue. A contrasting color was used on the small bag. Put some extra tissue around the gift in the bag and pull the ends up; out of the top.

3. Tie on the silk cording by looping around the handle (note the cording color is the same as the tissue for a super look!

4. Tie on two tassels (found in a fabric store) to the ends of the cording and the look is elegant!

5. In the large bag, the gift was wrapped in tissue and the ends pulled up and out from the top of the bag.

6. Part of the gift became the decoration when the two lace trimmed hand towels were formed into roses (see instruction below).

Hand Towel Roses

1. Each rose is made from a cotton hand towel with lace trim on one end. Tightly roll the bottom end of hand towel, (this roll will be the center of the flower.) When the roll is complete, secure between fingers and fold the towel in half, bringing the bottom and top ends together.

continued on inside back cover

CREATE-A-WRAP

*C*lever **Linda Lawrence** wraps her packages and makes tote bags using left over wallpaper! What a great idea. Wallpaper has a lot of body and makes strong tote bags!

*M*arsha **Ifland** has some great ideas for transforming a plain ordinary tote bag into something exceptional without a big expense!

TOWER OF TREATS

. . . .

Let your fingers do the "painting" on ordinary gift boxes for your own original designs.

MATERIALS NEEDED

Plain gift boxes
Acrylic paints for flowers
Squeeze bottle fabric paints for stems, leaves and flower centers
Shiny mylar ribbon

INSTRUCTIONS

1. Dip your finger in the acrylic paint and "finger paint" the flowers on the boxes (see illustration for the different strokes).

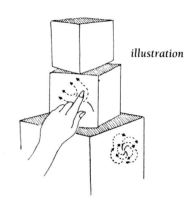

illustration

2. Draw in the leaves and stems with green squeeze bottle paint.

3. Add pink squeeze bottle paint to the flower centers, and to outline some of the petal shapes.

The packages look especially nice stacked and tied with shiny mylar ribbon.

LITTLE TREASURES

. . . .

When you decorate the lid of a box, instead of wrapping the entire box in paper, you can use it again and again.

MATERIALS NEEDED

3 complementary colors of pearl luster squeeze bottle fabric paints
Small scrap of floral fabric
Glue
Fine iridescent glitter
Strip of tulle netting for tie
Plain gift boxes

INSTRUCTIONS

1. Paint squeeze bottle fabric paint dots all over the lid of the box and tie a big bow of tulle netting.

2. For the floral box, cut a flower to fit your box from fabric and glue it to the lid. Rub your hands over the fabric to remove all the air bubbles and allow glue to dry.

3. Outline the flower and fill in the shaded areas on the fabric with different colors of squeeze bottle fabric paints. Match the paint colors to the fabric colors. Julie used dark green on the leaves, pink for the rose and light blue under the rose bud.

4. While the paint is still wet, sprinkle the design with very fine iridescent glitter and let dry about four hours. Shake off excess glitter and your box looks beautiful!

CREATE-A-WRAP

*M*arsha **Allen** turns
· ordinary gift boxes into
· a tower of floral treats
· filled with gifts!

*M*y sweet daughter, **Julie**
· **McGaha**, created these
· adorable gift boxes. A
· touch of pearl luster
· squeeze bottle fabric
· paints and a flower cut
· from fabric and you
· have a wonderful yet
· simple gift wrap!

PONGE PAINT

· · · · · · · · · · · · · · ·

You will have a great time printing the design on your own wrapping paper. Just cut out your favorite shape from a sponge and get started!

MATERIALS NEEDED

Ordinary sponges
Acrylic paints
Squeeze bottle paints
Fine glitter
Shiny white wrapping paper
Fine-tipped ink pen
Small amount of French wired ribbon
Several sprigs of fresh lavender

INSTRUCTIONS

1. Cut the sponges into your favorite shapes.
2. Wrap the box in shiny white paper so you know where to place the design.
3. Dip the sponge in acrylic paint and press the shape onto the paper.

4. Add squeeze paint for the perfect touch. With the fish, Marsha drew in a few waves of pink and green with some pink bubbles. You can sprinkle on fine glitter while the paint is still wet if you'd like.

5. After printing on the heart shapes, embellish with a tiny ribbon and bow drawing using a fine-tipped ink pen.

6. Tie on color coordinated ribbon. The French wired ribbon on the heart box is fun to work with. Slip in a few sprigs of fresh lavender and you have an extraordinary gift presentation!

RIBBONS FOR HER HAIR

· · · · · · · · · · · · · · ·

Colorful ribbons for her hair are special for every little girl. You con make this barrette for gifts as well as to decorate a box!

MATERIALS NEEDED

1 metal barrette base
1 ¹/₂ yards each of the three colors of ¹/₂" wide featheredge ribbon
Color coordinated wrapping paper
Wire

INSTRUCTIONS

1. Wrap your package in a paper color coordinated to the ribbons you use for your barrette.

2. Tie the ribbons around the box with the knot at the top. Leave the ribbon ends about 4" long.

3. Remove the tension spring from the metal barrette base. (Ask for instructions at the craft store where you purchase the supplies.)

4. Lay all three ribbons on top of one another. Leave an 8" tail of ribbon then wrap the thin wire 3 times around the barrette base and ribbons to secure.

5. Make a ribbon loop about l" long and wrap with a continuous length of wire. Continue making loops and wrapping with wire until the loops go all the way to the opposite side of the barrette. (See illustration.)

illustration

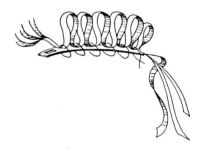

6. Wrap the wire and tie securely. Leave an 8" tail of ribbon. Cut all ends on the diagonal.

7. Return the tension spring to the inside of the barrette and clip on to the package just above the knot. Tie on if necessary with one of the 4" ribbon ends on the box.

Any little girl would love this barrette!

CREATE-A-WRAP

*M*arsha Ifland has a flair for creating sensational gift wrap that you are sure to love! She cut fish and heart shapes from ordinary everyday sponges, dipped them in paint, and "stamped" the print on shiny white paper.

*W*hat a treat to find an adorable ribbon barrette in the place of a bow on this little girl's package. The project is quick and easy, plus sure to please.

GARDEN PARTY
. . . .

Get out some old scissors, popsicle sticks and a hot glue gun, and make a darling picket fence for that extraordinary gift topper!

MATERIALS NEEDED
*Popsicle sticks
(we used 110 sticks
for a 12 x 14 fence)
White spray paint
Hot glue
Silk or fresh flower nosegay
Small round paper doily
Wire*

INSTRUCTIONS

1. Cut the popsicle sticks in half and trim one end of each stick to a point. (use an old pair of scissors.)
2. Lay two full-size popsicle sticks flat, about 1" apart. These become the horizontal fence rails.
3. Hot glue the pointed sticks to the horizontal fence rails, spacing them one stick apart. (Use an extra stick as a spacing guide.) Continue making these sections of fencing until you have enough for your decoration. Glue the sections together in the shape you like.

4. To make the arbor entrance, hot glue full-size popsicle sticks (or tongue depressor sticks) to the sides and top. You may have to cut a section in half, if necessary, so the arbor will fit.

5. To make the silk or fresh flower nosegay for the center of the garden, arrange the flowers together that complement your color scheme. Wrap with wire or florists tape to hold in place. Cut the stems off very short and slip a small round paper doily up under the flower heads. (If you are using fresh flowers, do this just before the event so the flowers look fresh.)

6. Hot glue the doily to the box to hold the flowers in place.

7. Hot glue the fence to the box to secure.

ODDS 'N ENDS
. . . .

Look around in your cupboards and you will be surprised at the unique and original gift decorations you will find!

MATERIALS NEEDED

*Small, unique odds and ends
Colorful wrapping paper
or boxes
Ribbon and doilies
Glue*

INSTRUCTIONS

1. Look through your cupboards and see what you have. Look with an eye for the unusual, pretty and colorful.

2. After wrapping your box, tie with ribbon. Marsha used French wire ribbon on the heart package and it added a rich touch.

3. Glue on your decoration. The tiny bird's nest looks charming on top of the gift and can be used again. The heart package has an essence of Victorian with the pop-up heart card and heart-shaped doilies glued to the top of the box.

Wonderful!

CREATE-A-WRAP

*C*an you believe that **Marsha Allen** made this delightful picket fence from popsicle sticks? The fence encloses a nosegay of fresh flowers and is a wonderful decoration for a special gift.

*M*arsha Ifland needed a gift wrapped in a hurry so she used odds and ends from around the house. She happened to have a tiny bird's nest and an old pop-up card. The gifts turned out absolutely charming!

UNDER THE SEA
. . . .

What do you do when the party is about to begin and you're out of wrapping paper? All is not lost if you have a pretty napkin!

MATERIALS NEEDED

Colorful print napkins
Matching paper plate
Ribbon

INSTRUCTIONS

1. Use one or two napkins to wrap your gift box, positioning the design on the front.

2. This package was tied with two leftover pieces of polypro-pylene ribbon. Wrap the corners of the box and tie in a knot. Shred the ends with a ribbon shredder. (See page 36 for shredder instructions.)

3. Cut the design from the center of the paper plate and punch a hole on the edge. Run a ribbon through and tie it onto the package.

Terrific!

WELCOME HOME
. . . .

The ideas are endless when you use doilies to decorate your gift boxes! They add a very feminine feeling to your design. Use your imagination. You might want to create a window with a flower box and lace curtains. Just cut the doily into whatever shape you like.

MATERIALS NEEDED

One large doily
A few scraps of white paper
Solid, colorful wrapping paper
Glue
Ribbon

INSTRUCTIONS

1. Wrap your box with the solid paper.

2. The large arched window over the door is a half circle cut from the center of the doily.

3. The door posts are strips of white paper covered with blue ribbon cut a little narrower than the paper (size them to fit your box proportions).

4. The squares on the door are cut from white paper.

5. The flowers, walkway, and other decorations were cut from the doily.

Have fun creating!

CREATE-A-WRAP

*C*his cute "fish" napkin
looks great as a gift
wrap, and how about
that name tag! It's cut
from the paper plate
that matches the
napkins!

*M*arsha Ifland designed
a beautiful Victorian
front door on her
package using a doily,
how clever this is! It
even has flowers
growing by the front
walkway.

MY LITTLE TOY DRUM

Don't throw away those large peanut cans, theater popcorn or take-out chicken containers! You can make a unique, whimsical container for gift-giving or to hold tiny cars or toys.

MATERIALS NEEDED

White paper
Large #5 size can
5 yards of ¹/₄"
wide red ribbon
1 yard of ¹/₂" wide gold ribbon
Red buttons (optional)
2 small dowels, each cut
9 ¹/₂" long
2 large wooden beads to fit on ends of dowels

INSTRUCTIONS

1. Wrap a strip of white paper all the way around the can and hot glue to hold.
2. Place ¹/₂"wide red ribbon in connected V shapes all the way around the container, hot gluing as you go (see photo).
3. Glue a ¹/₂"wide gold ribbon all the way around the top and bottom of the container.

4. Glue red buttons over the gold ribbon on the top and bottom of the can at each red ribbon V (see photo). Do not use the buttons if this is for a young child who might pull them off and put them in his or her mouth.

5. Criss-cross the two dowels and hot glue together for the drumsticks. Glue a large wooden bead to one end of each dowel. Place a large red pom-pom bow (see bow instructions on page 70) in the center of the drumsticks and glue to the lid of the can.

Delightful!

HOT OFF THE PRESS

The open-house section was used for the real estate salesman's gift (complete with an "open house" sign).

Add a few extra special touches to regular newspaper gift wrap and you have an appealing gift package.

MATERIALS NEEDED

Sheet music, newspapers, color comics
Tear-off strips from computer paper
Ribbon
Glue

INSTRUCTIONS

1. Choose the section in the newspaper that follows the interest of the one who will receive the gift, and wrap the box following the hints on page 24.
2. For the box wrapped in the stock quotations, we tied it with green ribbon (the color of money) and shredded the ends. Add some tear-off strips from the computer paper and the look is complete!
3. For the box using the real estate section, add a black bow and silver with purple mylar ribbon (see bow instructions on page 70). This bow has three loops on each side about 4" long. Cut the tail ribbon 8" long. Tie the bow to the package with a length of ribbon cut 16" long. If you are using two different ribbons, place one on top of the other, and treat as one ribbon as you make your bow. The element of surprise is the tiny "open house" sign stuck in the bow. Just cut out an open house ad from the classifieds and glue it to a toothpick.
4. Color comics have always been a great stand-by for a child's gift. They are still fun to use, but add a red pom-pom bow (see instructions on page 71) and paper dolls dancing around the top, and you have an awesome gift wrap!
5. To make the paper dolls, determine how long a strip of dolls you want. Cut the comics in a strip 2 ¹/₂" wide by the length you want. Fold the paper in half lengthwise. Then fold again and again until your paper is 2 ¹/₂" x 2". Cut the shape of the doll out of the paper. Be careful not to cut through the folded ends on the hands of the dolls (see illustration). Bend the feet over about ¹/₄" and glue to the top of the box.

Illustration

CREATE-A-WRAP

*C*lever **Marsha Allen** made this irresistible "drum" gift container from a large can! It can be used over and over to hold tiny treasures.

*T*he old stand-by of using newspaper when you're out of gift wrap has an updated look! Paper dolls can dance around the top of the box in color comics or the business section might wrap an executive's gift.

RESCUED BY FABRIC PAINT
. . . .

Have several colors of squeeze bottle paint on hand so you can be creative with your designs. You can get ideas from coloring books or gift cards.

MATERIALS NEEDED
Several colors of squeeze bottle fabric paint
Solid color wrapping paper
Ribbon (polypropylene for shredding)
Black pen

INSTRUCTIONS

1. Wrap the box in solid color paper and tie with ribbon.

2. The colorful balloons on Julie's yellow box appear as though they are flying! A few simple circles of squeeze bottle paint and a black pen to draw in the curling strings make a darling design. Add red ribbon and print "Happy Birthday" with yellow squeeze bottle paints. (**Hint:** add dots to the top and bottom plus where the lines join together on the letters to give a great look.)

3. The bow on the yellow box was made with polypropylene ribbon. There are three loops on each side about 2 ½" long. Cut the tail ribbon 5" long. Tie the bow with a 10" length of ribbon (see bow instructions on page 70). Tape the bow to the top left corner of the box.

4. We added ribbon "flowers" to the bow for a fun look. Use a ribbon shredder to make the "flowers." For each "flower" cut a length of 1" wide polypropylene ribbon 4 ½" long and another 3" long. To shred the ribbon, follow instructions that come with the small plastic ribbon shredder. (See page 36.) Begin shredding ½" in from the end and continue to within ½" of the other end of each ribbon. Fold the shredded 3" ribbon in half and join the two unshredded

ends together. Tightly roll the ends and tape together to hold. This forms the center of your "flower." Now fold the 4 ½" shredded ribbon in half and join the two unshredded ends together. Place the unshredded ends of the two ribbons side by side. Place the small ribbon you just completed as the "flower" center up against this folded ribbon. Roll the longer ribbon around the smaller one to complete the petals. Tape all of this securely together. (See illustration.)

Illustration

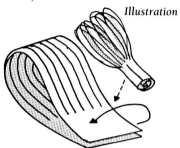

Glue or tape the "flower" onto the loops on the bow. We made three ribbon "flowers" to tuck in this bow. Shred the tail ends on the bow and you have a great package!

5. For the "big foot" box, Julie used red squeeze bottle paint on the white paper and white squeeze bottle paint on the red ribbon to make the footprints that march all over the box. The squeeze bottle paints are easy to work with. Just draw the shape of a tiny foot and put in dots for the toes. The footprints are even on the premade bow for a fun look! Wrap the box and tie the ribbon on. Then draw an outline of a large footprint, and cut out for the name tag. Cute!

USING SCRAPS
. . . .

Cut out the design for a delightful gift decoration when you only have a small scrap of wrapping paper.

MATERIALS NEEDED

Small scrap of wrapping paper
Ribbon
Plain gift box

INSTRUCTIONS

1. Cut out the design on the paper scrap and glue it to the box.

2. If you only have scraps of ribbons and they're not long enough to

tie around the box, wrap one of them all the way around the box and tape together to hold the box closed. Take any other ribbon scraps you have that complement the color scheme and tape them onto the back of the box. Bring the ends around to the front and form a loop. Tape or glue in place (see photo).

3. Cut the ribbon ends in a V shape and your gift package is complete!

CREATE-A-WRAP

*J*ulie Klinsky *grabs a bottle of squeeze bottle fabric paint when she needs to come up with a unique last minute gift wrap!*

*Y*ou're in a hurry to wrap a gift for your child to take to a party, and all you have is a small scrap of wrapping paper and a few inches of ribbon. Don't panic . . . we have the answer!

STENCIL IT

You only need a few supplies to stencil on a great design and put a finishing touch to your gift wrap.

MATERIALS NEEDED

All are at craft stores.
Stencil
Stencil brush
Oil paint sticks or
stencil crayons
1 yard twisted paper ribbon

INSTRUCTIONS

1. Your stenciling materials will come with instructions. A few pointers...use very little paint on your brush. The paint stencil crayons or paint sticks are great.

2. Use circular movements when applying the paint. To create a darker edge, push the brush up against the stencil edge. To create a softer edge, pull the brush into the center away from the stencil edge.

3. The ideas are endless with so many wonderful patterns available. Julie used 2 different sized hearts and the small bunny from one stencil sheet on her tote bag.

4. The tag is cut from a grocery bag and stenciled. The tag edges have just a hint of color brushed on them. Punch a hole and hang the tag from a pretty ribbon.

5. The large bow is made from 1 yard of twisted paper ribbon. Untwist the ribbon and form into loops and wire to hold. Wire to handle. Julie says the printing on the tote bag is easy to do with a fat-tip pen. She put dots at the top and bottom and where the lines join together...practice that one!

6. The lambs stenciled on a grocery bag look terrific for a baby gift. Julie folded over a paper scrap and stenciled on a lamb. After cutting it out with the fold at the top, she had a great tag for her gift.

7. The ribbons are fun. I found a great variety of ribbons for children at the ribbon store. I mixed "happy faces" and "kids" ribbon together for a great touch to the package.

UNIQUE GIFT TAGS

Use what ever you have on hand to make a personal tag for your gift. Don't throw away scraps of ribbon or whatever you have used in a decorating project. Keep a box for scraps so you can pull from it to make up something original!

MATERIALS NEEDED

3x5 Cards
String tags
Peel-off labels
Stickers, marking pens
Doilies
Construction paper
Ribbon

INSTRUCTIONS

1. Cut a 3 x 5 card in half...put a sticker in the corner ...cut around the outside edge of the sticker...punch a hole in the opposite end...tie a tiny ribbon through the hole...and you have a wonderful name tag for a gift!

2. How about stenciling the half of a 3 x 5 card with a Christmas tree, making a tiny line border all the way around with a gold pen, punching a hole in the corner and loop a gold cord onto the tag. A "Merry Christmas" written in gold ink completes the look!

3. Take a small peel-off label, add a tiny flower sticker to the top left corner, draw a few gold lines around the edge, and the tag looks great. Note how Marsha breaks the gold lines and where she places them.

4. See what you can do with inexpensive string tags. Take off the string, add a satin ribbon, a tiny flower and a line border. You have a darling gift tag!

5. The fold-over cards were made with construction paper. On the pink card, paper doilies were cut into sections and glued in a collage effect to the front. A flower was cut from a scrap of wrapping paper and glued on top.

6. A doily was used as a stencil for a fold-over card. Just place the doily on the front of the construction paper card and use a stencil brush and stencil paintsticks to create this look.

Great ideas for quick, easy and custom gift tags!

CREATE-A-WRAP

*C*lever **Julie Klinsky**
enjoys stenciling her
packages. Here she
dressed up a plain
brown tote bag to look
terrific. And look what
lamb stencils did to a
brown paper bag!
Stenciling is
Fast...Fun...and Easy!

*M*arsha Ifland enjoys
making original gift
tags for her friends.
We have pictured some
of her great ideas for
you.

RIBBONS

Simple to do, yet looks tremendous! Short strips of ribbons that you couldn't bear to throw away can be put to good use!

MATERIALS NEEDED

Ribbon scraps
Tape
Glue
Plain gift boxes

INSTRUCTIONS

1. Weave short pieces of ribbon in and out, and tape on the inside of the lid as you go along. No need for paper or a bow!

2. Gold wrapping paper cut into strips was used on the small box. Just weave them in and out and tape on the inside of the lid as you go. I happened to have a short piece of beautiful lamé floral ribbon. It was too short to tie in a bow, so I tied it in a slip knot on the side of the box! Super!

SIMPLE ELEGANCE

Keep your gift wrap cupboard stocked with solid color paper and matching ribbons plus beautiful stickers, and you can create a captivating gift wrap in a moment's notice!

MATERIALS NEEDED

Solid color wrapping paper
2 yards of ribbon
Victorian sticker
One fresh rose

INSTRUCTIONS

1. Wrap your box with beautiful colored paper.

2. Tie the ribbon around the box by beginning in the center on the top. Leave a ribbon tail of about 6". Wrap the ribbon around the box twice. Tie in a knot, making sure the tie ends go under the second ribbon on the box to pull it all together at the top.

3. Place a large Victorian sticker on the bottom left side of the box. Tuck in a sweet smelling flower and it's ready to brighten someone's day!

CREATE-A-WRAP

*S*ylvia Eckhardt saves ribbon and uses all the short pieces to create a basket weave look for her gift boxes! Mix coordinating colors together for an inter-esting appeal.

*M*arsha Ifland decorated this darling package in a jiffy using a few simple items for a sweet, fresh look!

GONE FISHING

· · · · · · · · · · · ·

You will have fun making up this gift wrap! Collect a few things together and get ready to create!

MATERIALS NEEDED

*Wrapping paper
that reminds you
of water
Bow and ribbon to match
Gold shredded mylar strips
(these come in a package)
Chopsticks
for fishing poles
Metal bobbins with white
thread for reels
Small straw hat
Fishing flies*

INSTRUCTIONS

1. Wrap your box and tie with matching ribbons and bow. Tie gold shredded mylar strips under the bow for dazzle.

2. Hot glue the metal bobbins to the ends of the chopsticks for fishing reels. Glue the poles to the package with a bead of hot glue.

3. The small straw hat came from a craft store. Hot glue it to the box and stick the new "flies" into the hat. You can add a miniature fishing box if you like.
A unique gift wrap!

BLOCK PRINT

· · · · · · · · · · · ·

You can make up a terrific gift wrapping paper with a sponge and paint!

MATERIALS NEEDED

*Brown mailing paper
Twine
Curling ribbon
Black felt tip pen
Sponge
Acrylic paint
Golf tees*

INSTRUCTIONS

1. Wrap the box in the brown paper so you will know where to print on the box.

2. Cut out the shape you want from an ordinary sponge. Dip it in the acrylic paint and "print" it on the brown paper.

3. Put the finishing touch with a felt tip pen as Marsha did on the golf balls and hearts (see photo).

4. Add some twine or curling ribbon. Tie on some golf tees and a name tag.

Original and fast . . . fun and easy.

CREATE-A-WRAP

$\mathcal{M}$arsha **Allen** is "reel-ing" in the compli-ments with this smashing gift wrap for the fisherman in her life!

$\mathcal{M}$arsha **Ifland**'s hus-band is an avid golfer so she customized a package to fit his sport. She also "printed" the heartshaped balloons on brown mailing paper . . . fabulous!

BASIC BOW

This bow can be tricky to make if this is your first attempt. The secret is to practice, so don't give up if the bow slips out of your hand and you have to start over. My first bow was a disaster but I kept trying until I finally made a perfect bow. You can do it too...just follow these simple instructions.

1. Hold the ribbon right side up between your thumb and index finger. Pinch the ribbon approximately 2″ from the end and then form a loop as large as you need, rolling the ribbon up and away from you. Place the long end of the ribbon between your thumb and index finger to create the bow's center (*see illustration #1*).

Illustration #1

Illustration #2

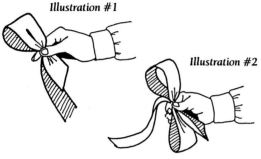

2. Before making the bottom loop, make a half twist to the left so that the ribbon will be right side out, then roll the ribbon down and away from you. Pinch the ribbon together at the bow's center (*see illustration #2*).

3. Continue making the loops until the desired number is reached, keeping the loop sizes the same. Remember to ALWAYS pinch the ribbon at the center and to ALWAYS twist to the left before forming each loop.

> HINT: To keep the bow from slipping, lift your index finger as you twist, momentarily using your middle finger and thumb to secure the loops until the twist is completed.

4. Once the loops are completed, cut the end of the ribbon leaving a tail as long as required (this length will vary on each design). Now you are ready to wire.

5. To secure the bow, tie a piece of wire around the bow's center and twist the wire ends tightly together underneath the bow. Now arrange the loops to form a perfect bow.

6. Cut a length of ribbon (exact size will be given in each design instructions) to create your "tie" for the bow. Wrap the tie around the bow's center to conceal the florists wire and knot the ribbon in the back.

7. All ends of the ribbon should be cut on the diagonal or in a "V" shape.

FLORISTS BOW

1. This bow is made exactly the same as the BASIC BOW except begin by pinching the ribbon between your thumb and index finger 4″ from the end.

2. Proceed with the instructions for the BASIC BOW until all the desired loops are formed. Before you secure the bow with wire, twist the 4″ end on top of the bow, making sure the right side is out. Curl this end around and place it under your thumb. Place the wire through the small center loop, taking care to catch the end in the center loop (*see illustration #1*).

Illustration #1

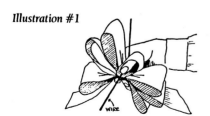

3. Arrange loops to form a perfect bow. Cut a length of ribbon to create your "tie" for the bow. Place the tie ribbon through this small center loop and knot in the back.

TIE BOW

1. This bow is the one used on the back of little girls' dresses, around your neck, shoe laces, packages, etc. Follow these simple instructions and you will tie a perfect bow every time.

2. Starting with both ends even, cross the right ribbon underneath the left (This is very important to keep the bow straight). Make a half-knot as shown in illustration #1.

Illustration #1

Illustration #2

3. With left hand make a loop between the thumb and index finger, keeping the wrong sides of the ribbon together. Cross over the top of the loop with the other ribbon right side up. Now finish the second loop by pulling it up through the center space you've just created. Pull tight.

> HINT: To prevent the wrong side out on the second loop, twist ribbon a half-turn just before sending it up through the center space (*see illustration #2*). If the right tail is wrong side out, twist the left loop and the right tail towards you simultaneously in a rolling motion.

POMPOM BOW

The average pompom bow requires 3 ½ yards of ribbon. Add more to tie on the box.

1. Form a loop of ribbon about 6" across. (Adjust the size of the loop for a larger or smaller bow.)

2. Wrap the ribbon around loop twenty times for an extra full bow.

3. Flatten the loops and cut off triangles at each end. (see illustration #1).

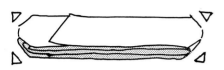

Illustration #1

4. Bring the ends together in the middle, matching the cut triangles. (see illustration #2).

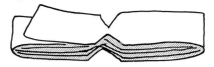

Illustration #2

5. Wrap the center where the cut triangles come together with wire. Pull out the loops by holding the bow in your left hand and pulling all the loops toward the center and twisting with your right hand. When one side is complete, reverse sides and continue pulling out and twisting the loops with the right hand to form the pompom bow.

WRAPPING HINTS
continued from page 24

LID:

1. Place the lid on the paper and measure the amount needed to cover the top. Include the sides plus the overlap edges all the way around. Cut the paper to size.

2. Turn the paper wrong side up and place the lid upside down in the center. Bring the paper up and over the two long sides, and tape the overlapped edges to the inside of the lid, clipping the paper at the corners so it will fit nicely (see illustration #1).

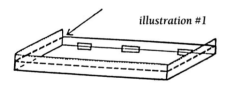

illustration #1

3. Miter the corners on the ends of the lid and fold up and over the side and tape to the inside of the lid (see illustration #2).

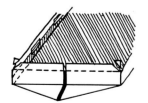

illustration #2

BOX:

1. Place the box on the paper and measure the amount needed to cover the box, including all four sides plus a 1" overlap on the top.

2. Turn the paper wrong side up and place the box in the center. Bring the paper up and over the long sides of the box and follow the instruction #2 and #3 above. Run your fingers around all the edges of the box and lid to give a sharp creased finished look.

ITEMS TO HAVE ON HAND:

Always buy color coordinated paper and ribbon so if you run short of paper you can use scraps from different patterns. Keep a special cupboard for wrapping supplies with paper, lots of ribbons, double-sided or transparent tape, scissors, glue, stickers, squeeze bottle fabric paint, doilies, 3 x 5 cards, hole punch, stapler and you will be ready for a quick wrap anytime!

It has been our intention to bring you a great book on creative gift wrapping. Many of the people who have contributed to this book have made the comment, "this book has everything but the kitchen sink!" Well, since we wanted it to have EVERYTHING . . . we have included the kitchen sink just for fun!!

We hope this book has been helpful to you, and that you enjoyed looking through the pages and pages of ideas. We wanted it to be beautiful and also fun. We hope you are pleased!

SHIRTS-N-TIES
continued from page 10

3. Cut the tie from a paper of your choice. See illustration #2 for the shape to cut. Size it to fit your box proportions.

Illustration #2

4. Slip the knot end of the tie under the center of the collar and glue in place.

5. Glue down the center of the collar over the tie. Glue the buttons on the collar points...What a great package!

Brown ribbon box
MATERIALS NEEDED

Bold color wrapping paper
2 ½ yards of brown twist paper ribbon

INSTRUCTIONS

1. After wrapping with a bold color paper, measure around the box for the length of ribbon needed. Be sure to add 14" to your measurement for the knot and tie ends. Cut the twisted paper ribbon the correct length needed.

2. Untwist the paper ribbon, leaving 2" of each end still tightly twisted. Tie around the box as described in step #1, with the knot in the center front of the box, pulling the tie ends out to the sides.

3. Cut two pieces of twisted paper ribbon 6" long and untwist to within 2" of one end on each piece. Tuck the untwisted ends under the knot and tape or glue in place. (See illustration.) Terrific!

Illustration

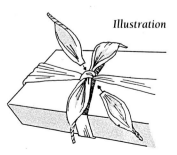

SUMMER TIME
continued from page 34

the flowers are growing where you want them. You can leave several flowers open in full circles and glue onto the box.

5. Draw the rest of your garden on the box with colored marking pens. Add some colorful tape for a rainbow effect if you like.

FLOWER BASKET
continued from page 40

7. Begin by attaching the fabric strip to the lower edge of the handle on the side using hot glue to secure. Continue up the side of the handle and form a loop. Hot glue in place. Pull the fabric across the top of the handle to the center point, and form the bow loops as shown in illustration #1.

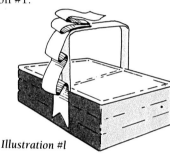

Illustration #1

8. Repeat the process on the other side of the handle using the second strip of fabric. Cut off any excess fabric at the center point and reserve to use later to create a knot effect. Hot glue the fabric ends in the center to the handle.

9. Place paper cups or paper towel cardboard tubes in the centers of the bow loops to hold their shape until dry.

10. Wrap a piece of fabric across the bow in the center to create a knot effect (use the fabric cut from the excess in the center of the bow). Pull the fabric down around the handle and overlap, holding in place with hot glue. Allow to dry completely before removing paper cups. Tuck in a color coordinated gift and you have a spectacular presentation!

WALLPAPER TOTE BAG
continued from page 50

Wallpaper Totes
MATERIALS NEEDED

A piece of wallpaper
(20 ¾" x 16")
1 yard of ribbon,
yarn, cord, jute or
light rope for the handle.

INSTRUCTIONS

1. The width of the wallpaper is 20 ¾", cut the length 16" long (the finished bag will be 6 ½" wide x 12" high).

2. With the right side up, measure down 1 ½" from the top, and fold back so the two wrong sides are together. Run your fingers over the fold to make a sharp crease, and then unfold. If you want a border at the top of your bag, add it now. Glue it on just under the fold line, across the full 20 ¾" width of the paper (see illustration#1).

3. Measure 2 ½" from the bottom, and fold the paper back so the two wrong sides are together. Run your finger over the fold to make a sharp crease and then unfold (see illustration #1).

4. Measure off the following increments across the width of the paper, and mark as you go. Begin on the left side and measure across to the right side of the paper (see illustration#1). Measure and mark 6 ½" (in from the left side) + 1 ¾" + 1 ¾" + 6 ½" + 1 ¾" + 1 ¾" (you will have a ¼" edge remaining on the right hand side).

Illustration #1

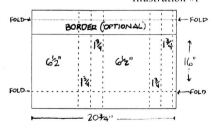

The height of the bags can vary by increasing or decreasing the distance between the top and bottom fold (The top 1 ½" and the bottom 2 ½" fold overs always remain the same).

continued